YOUR KNOWLEDGE HAS VALUE

- We will publish your bachelor's and master's thesis, essays and papers

- Your own eBook and book - sold worldwide in all relevant shops

- Earn money with each sale

Upload your text at www.GRIN.com
and publish for free

Bibliographic information published by the German National Library:

The German National Library lists this publication in the National Bibliography; detailed bibliographic data are available on the Internet at http://dnb.dnb.de .

This book is copyright material and must not be copied, reproduced, transferred, distributed, leased, licensed or publicly performed or used in any way except as specifically permitted in writing by the publishers, as allowed under the terms and conditions under which it was purchased or as strictly permitted by applicable copyright law. Any unauthorized distribution or use of this text may be a direct infringement of the author s and publisher s rights and those responsible may be liable in law accordingly.

Imprint:

Copyright © 2017 GRIN Verlag, Open Publishing GmbH
Print and binding: Books on Demand GmbH, Norderstedt Germany
ISBN: 9783668582194

This book at GRIN:

http://www.grin.com/en/e-book/382077/the-adaption-of-cmmi-for-an-in-house-software-development-department

Rehan Shabbir

The Adaption of CMMI for an In-House Software Development Department

GRIN Publishing

GRIN - Your knowledge has value

Since its foundation in 1998, GRIN has specialized in publishing academic texts by students, college teachers and other academics as e-book and printed book. The website www.grin.com is an ideal platform for presenting term papers, final papers, scientific essays, dissertations and specialist books.

Visit us on the internet:

http://www.grin.com/

http://www.facebook.com/grincom

http://www.twitter.com/grin_com

Adaption of CMMI by Software Development Department

Rehan Shabbir Khan
Virtual University of Pakistan
July, 2017

ABSTRACT

This paper is a basic work for introducing the CMMI for in-house software development department. The purpose of this paper is to develop a ground and a clear understanding for the organizations who are willing to adapt the best practices in general for increasing the functional and technical efficiency at their in-house software development department.

Normally the CMMI is implemented at organization level in the software development, software engineering, system engineering or system security organizations. The main theme of this paper is to attain CMMI level-2 in software development department.

Once the best practices become common in an organization at departmental level, that opens new horizons to build high level understanding of more mature and simplified set of processes that leads toward the organizational maturity which covers the set of overall process areas across the organization.

There are various factors involve that limits an organization to adopt a process improvement model. Usually the new emerging organizations having the staff who have previous experience in highly functioning organizations plan to adapt the process improvement models. It is also a dilemma that small and medium size organizations could not establish successful implementation of Software improvement process models because such organizations work in limited resources and restrict time frame [1]. It is more hard to adapt the CMMI at departmental level because main focus of such an organization is towards the productivity or the main stream of the business. The In-house software development departments are always work in the capacity of supporting department that facilitate and develop the software and systems for the main business of the organization. Therefore, budget constraints and lack of resources exist in such environments. Although, technology is developed and used by all departments and branches within the organization, however, there may be the communication gap between software development department and other units of the organization [1].

Specifically, this paper will provide the structural process and case study of software development department of an organization having very diversified functional and financial dimensions to improve functional efficiency from poorly controlled activities to a managed environment or in short achieving the CMMI maturity level-2.

Keywords: Department level CMMI, Process Improvement, Process maturity, CMMI Level-2

Table of Contents

1. INTRODUCTION 4
2. HISTORY OF CMMI 6
3. CMMI COMPONENTS 6
4. BENEFITS OF CMMI 6
5. CASE STUDY OF 'AKHUWAT' 6
   5.1   Requirements Management 7
   5.2   Project Planning 7
   5.3   Project Monitoring and Control 7
   5.4   Measurement and Analysis 8
   5.5   Process Quality Assurance 8
   5.6   Configuration Management 8
6. FUTURE WORK 8
7. CONCLUSION 9
8. REFERENCES 10

1. INTRODUCTION

Just like Information Technology Infrastructure Library, the Capability Maturity Model Integration is not a standard or set of processes and procedures, rather it is a collection of best practices that has been collected from highly functioning organizations. These best practices are not supposed to be implement in all organizations in same way rather these are adjustable in local environment of an organization and very useful to take measures in improving the processes and activates.

The maturity levels are well defined evolutionary plateau to measure the improvement in processes and activities of an organization.

The CMMI level two is termed as 'Managed' and at this level process characterized for project is often reactive but in very smart and efficient way. CMMI helps the organization to set process improvement goals and priorities.

This paper also includes the case study that was structured to address the process areas like Requirements Management, Project Planning, Project Monitoring and Control, Measurement and Analysis, Process Quality Assurance, Configuration Management as defined by the CMMI level-2.

Although, higher CMM levels enhance the project performance and software quality as well as reduces the software development efforts and timelines [2], but a lower maturity level is a pre-requisite for the next level and provides a necessary foundation for implementing processes of a higher level [5].

Following are the big names that are using CMMI;

Boeing, BMW, Ericsson, Fujitsu, Hitachi, Honeywell, KPMG, Intel, Motorola, NEC, Nokia, Samsung [5].

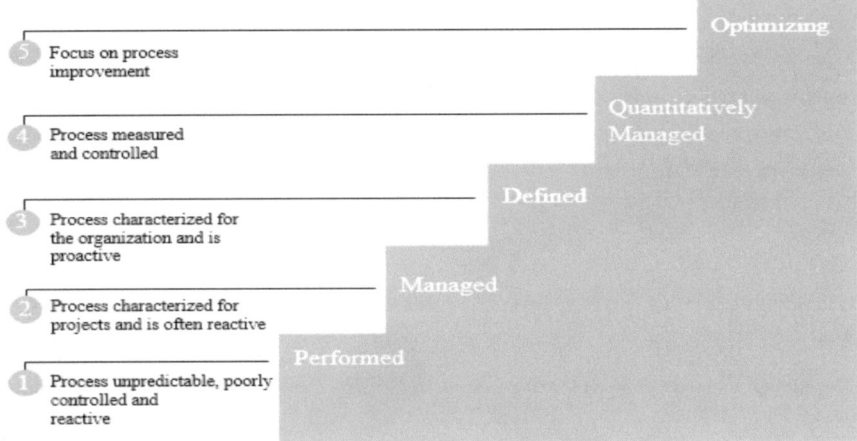

Figure-1, CMMI Staged Maturity Levels

Year	Description
2001	Version 1.1 of CMMI
2002	Implementation guide for government evaluation was published.
2004	CMMI for acquisition module was published.

Table-1, CMMI History [5]

2. HISTORY OF CMMI

With the induction of CMMI in the industry, the Capability Maturity Model Integration is known as the best practices model. It covered the best practices in the disciplines of System Engineering (SE), Software Engineering (SW), Supplier and Sourcing (SS), Integrated Process and Product Development (IPPD). [6]

3. CMMI COMPONENTS

Compatibility Maturity Model Integration is available in two representations that are 'Staged' and 'Continuous'.

Staged representation grouped the process areas (PA) in to maturity levels as shown in figure-1 [6].

Continuous representation assesses the capability level of individual process area (PA). [7]

Each representation has sub-division called Process Areas (PA). Each process area has set of generic and specific best practices called Generic Goals (GGs) and Specific Goals (SGs) [6].

Generic Goals (GG) and Specific Goals (SG) are the integral parts of Process Areas. Generic goals apply to all process areas and the Specific goals apply to a particular process area. Generic goals deal with the institutionalization and implementation of process areas and the Specific Goals defines the unique characteristics to satisfy the purpose of the process area and generalize the strategies to achieve the goals [8].

4. BENEFITS OF CMMI

CMMI provides an integrated common strategic vision in a modeled way for the improvements in processes. It significantly increases the impact of productivity and functional improvement. It increases quality and customer satisfaction. Improves the morale of employees and increases return on investments. It decreases the cost of quality and help to predict the budgets [5].

5. CASE STUDY OF 'AKHUWAT'

'Akhuwat' is an emerging organization that works to alleviate poverty through interest free microfinance, education, capacity building and social guidance in Pakistan. In June 2017, it has more than five thousand employees and 686 operational branch offices. It has disbursed PKR 43.727 Billion in 2.039 Million families with recovery rate of 99.94%. It is the largest and fastest growing MFI in Pakistan.

[http://akhuwat.org.pk/progress_report.asp]

To meet the technology challenges 'Akhuwat' stablished data center, acquired ERP System, setup software development department and arrange an in-house build of MIS for managing its operations. However, there were no IT processes there and the internal functions were poorly controlled.

This paper includes the case study of requirement assessment and implementation of CMMI level-2 for The Software Development Department of Akhuwat.

5.1 Requirements Management

At the initial stages there was a there was a single part time developer at Akhuwat. The software development department was stablished and development of credit management system was started without any processes. In due course budgets were allotted for the department for capacity building, making processes, user trainings and for software process improvement. A fully qualified software development team was hired; Detailed list of requirements were setup. Processes and policies were defined and working hierarchies were structured to manage and monitor the functions and activities.

5.2 Project Planning

The trend of project planning was introduced in software development department. Resource planning, cost analysis, functional requirements, hardware requirements, operational processes, trainings, timeline and schedule are the main components of project planning.

5.3 Project Monitoring and Control

Project monitoring and control tools and techniques were adopted. Project management criteria and polices were defined.

5.4 Measurement and Analysis

Processes and resources were gathered and estimated. The compatibility of plans with current status was determined. Limitations and root causes were identified for improvement.

5.5 Process Quality Assurance

It has been strictly followed that only the planned and predefined processes are followed because the process quality assurance provides the stability to the department, decreases the unexpected delays and results in high quality products. Group of shared resources was provided the role of process quality assurance to accommodate the cost of the projects.

5.6 Configuration Management

Service asset and configuration management was implemented to ensure that the required assets are properly controlled to deliver the services and reliable information about those assets are accurately documented. Configuration management identify, control and verify the services and other configuration items to ensure the integrity and completeness of configuration documentation.

6. FUTURE WORK

There is a need to research and develop the model in compliance with CMMI level-2 to maintain the processes for a section of an organization that will enhance the polices up to advance level. It must be realized that investment on technology and development is essential to survive. It fastens the processes, brings accuracy and returns in a long run. The plans and policies should be documented properly and adhere these policies. CMMI level-2 requires that appropriate assignment of responsibility and authority must be maintained. People will be well trained and configuration items will be managed. The use of tools and techniques would be implemented to monitor and control the process performance. Certain measuring initiatives should be taken to review the processes, work products and services. There should be proper procedure for process reviewing, redesigning and simplifying to meet the requirement and minimizing the process time.

7. CONCLUSION

This research work contributes towards to methodological and practical application of Compatibility Maturity Model Integration for the organization that are moving to adapt CMMI model in the disciplines of System Engineering (SE), Software Engineering (SW), Supplier and Sourcing (SS), Integrated Process and Product Development (IPPD).

It is the time of bits and bauds, time is now measured in Micro and Nano seconds. Now it is not the question that, have you have move on the new technology or not? It is now asked that how frequently you are adapting the change. In this fast growing technology era there is a need of structuring and modeling the organizational units. It's the question of survival. If some organization with not strengthen its software development department and structure it on the basis of derived methodologies and best practices, it will not survive in near future.

CMMI is one of the most appropriate and compatible model to be implemented in software development department and provides an integrated common strategic vision up to required maturity level in a modeled way for the improvements in processes.

----

8. REFERENCES

1. Software SMEs' unofficial readiness for CMMI_-based software process improvement
   Javed Iqbal1, Rodina Binti Ahmad1, Mohd Hairul Nizam, Md Nasir, Mahmood Niazi, Shahaboddin Shamshirband, Muhammad Asim Noor.

2. Impact of CMMI-Based Process Maturity Levels on Effort, Productivity and Diseconomy of Scale
   Majed Alyahya, Rodina Ahmad, and Sai Peck Lee
   Department of Software Engineering, University of Malaya, Malaysia

3. A comparative analysis of CMMI software project management by Brazilian, Indian and Chinese companies
   Saulo Barbara´ de Oliveira, Rogerio Valle, Cla´udio Fernando Mahler

4. Evaluating the service quality of software providers appraised in CMM/CMMI
   Rodrigo Pinheiro dos Santos, Kathia Marcal de Oliveira, Wander Pereira da Silva

5. Capability Maturity Model® Integration (CMMI®) Overview
   Sponsored by the U.S. Department of Defense © 2005 by Carnegie Mellon University

6. PEM: The small company-dedicated software process quality evaluation method combining CMMISM and ISO/IEC 14598
   Sylvie Trudel, Jean-Marc Lavoie, Marie-Claude Par´e, Witold Suryn

7. Towards a CMMI-Compliant Goal-Oriented Software Process through Model-Driven Development
   Alexandre Marcos Lins de Vasconcelos, Giovanni Giachetti, Beatriz Marín, and Oscar Pastor

8. A service innovation framework for start-up firms by integrating service experience engineering approach and capability maturity model
   K. J. Wang, J. Widagdo, Y. S. Lin, H. L. Yang, S. L. Hsiao

YOUR KNOWLEDGE HAS VALUE

- We will publish your bachelor's and master's thesis, essays and papers

- Your own eBook and book - sold worldwide in all relevant shops

- Earn money with each sale

Upload your text at www.GRIN.com
and publish for free